In the Waiting

publishing team

Director, Student Ministry
Ben Trueblood

Manager, Student Ministry Publishing
John Paul Basham

Editorial Team Leader
Karen Daniel

Writer
Jennifer Dixon

Content Editor
Stephanie Cross

Production Editor
Brooke Hill

Graphic Designer
Kaitlin Redmond

©2021 Lifeway Press®

No part of this work may be reproduced or transmitted in any form or by any means, electronic or mechanical, including photocopying and recording, or by any information storage or retrieval system, except as may be expressly permitted in writing by the publisher. Requests for permission should be addressed in writing to LifeWay Press®, One LifeWay Plaza, Nashville, TN 37234.

ISBN 978-1-0877-4433-9
Item 005831821
Dewey Decimal Classification Number: 242
Subject Heading: DEVOTIONAL LITERATURE / BIBLE STUDY AND TEACHING / GOD

Printed in the United States of America

Student Ministry Publishing
LifeWay Resources
One LifeWay Plaza
Nashville, Tennessee 37234

We believe that the Bible has God for its author; salvation for its end; and truth, without any mixture of error, for its matter and that all Scripture is totally true and trustworthy. To review LifeWay's doctrinal guideline, please visit www.lifeway.com/doctrinalguideline.

Unless otherwise noted, all Scripture quotations are taken from the Christian Standard Bible®, Copyright © 2017 by Holman Bible Publishers. Used by permission. Christian Standard Bible® and CSB® are federally registered trademarks of Holman Bible Publishers.

table of contents

04 intro

05 getting started

06 what does the Bible teach about patience?

16 the vital virtue of patience

30 God's patience toward us

44 why does God make me wait?

58 how to be patient

66 while you wait

76 in pursuit of patience

Intro

We live in a fast-paced, fast-food, instant-posting, instant-message, one-click-ordering world. We want what we want, the way we want it—and in the exact moment we begin to desire it, we want it delivered. Psychologists have labeled this no-wait tendency as *instant gratification*. When we don't feel fulfilled in some way, we actually become tense and anxious.[1]

Ask your grandparents, or even your parents, about what it was like to have to wait for a newspaper to be delivered or the evening news to find out what was going on in the world. We don't really know what that's like because we depend on the instantaneous sharing through smart phones and social media. Honestly, there's just not much we have to wait for, so when we do have to wait or be patient, it can feel excruciating.

While a need and expectation for things to occur in a timely manner is neither wrong nor unhealthy, assuming that things will happen right now in life as they do in our digital worlds has grossly misconstrued our perception of what it means to have patience. To learn what patience truly is, we can't look around us or even back to previous generations. Truly understanding patience requires us to know God and to know who we are in relation to Him.

Patience isn't something we're left alone to discover, though; God leads us to understanding through His Word and the indwelling of His Holy Spirit. Over the next 30 days, we'll pursue patience as we search God's Word for answers. We'll dig deep into what the Bible teaches about patience, how God is patient with us, why it seems that God often makes us wait, and how we can become patient people, too.

As you spend time getting to know your Creator, you'll see what's going on in the waiting and how you can respond.

getting started

This devotional contains 30 days of content, broken down into sections about patience. Each day is divided into three elements—discover, delight, and display—to help you answer core questions related to Scripture.

discover

This section helps you examine the passage in light of who God is and determine what it says about your identity in relationship to Him. Included here is the daily Scripture reading, focus passage, along with illustrations and commentary to guide you as you explore God's Word.

delight

In this section, you'll be challenged by questions and activities that help you see how God is alive and active in every detail of His Word and your life.

display

Here's where you take action. Display calls you to apply what you've learned through each day's study.

prayer

Each day also includes a prayer activity in one of the three main sections.

Throughout the devotional, you'll also find extra articles and activities to help you connect with the topic personally, such as such as Scripture memory verses, additional resources, and questions.

day 1

DO GOOD, BE PATIENT

discover

READ GALATIANS 6:7-10.

Let us not get tired of doing good, for we will reap at the proper time if we don't give up. —Galatians 6:9

We all like to see the rewards of doing a task that requires our time and commitment. If we study for a test, we like to be rewarded with a good grade. If we practice a dance or a song, we like to see improvement in our ability on stage. Everyone wants to see a good return wherever they invest their time and talents.

When we do good for others, we may not see benefit for a long time. But Paul said that "God is not mocked. For whatever a man sows he will also reap" (v. 7). In these words, we have assurance that God sees the good we are doing and that He will reward us. He comforts us, explaining that our good deeds are not in vain. Good deeds will be rewarded in the "proper time," which means they are not going to be rewarded in "our time." But we can trust that a time will come when our good deeds *will* be rewarded.

As believers in a good and just God, we have the assurance that God will make use of the good we do. So, we should continue working for the good of others even when we are tempted to stop because we don't see major results. We trust that our rewards are from God and not from what we can see, and we know that doing good for others and being patient go together.

delight |

When do you get discouraged from doing good? Where does your discouragement come from?

God promises He will reward the good you do. How does His promise encourage you to be patient with the process, especially when you don't see the results?

display |

Think of the last time you quit or were tempted to quit doing good for a girl you know because you got discouraged. Journal the reasons you did not want to do good in that situation. Now, beside those reasons, answer the question: *What can I do instead of abandoning what is right?*

Memorize Galatians 6:9 as a reminder to persevere when it's tough to do good.

> **Thank God that He notices every act of kindness—even those that seem small to us. Tell Him about when you get discouraged and why you want to stop doing good for others at times. Ask for His help to remain faithful and patient, to keep doing good even when you want to quit.**

day 2

REMAINING HOPEFUL

discover

READ ROMANS 8:18-25.

Now if we hope for what we do not see, we eagerly wait for it with patience.
—Romans 8:25

We all have a sense deep down inside us that this world is not what it should be. What is a girl to do with the disappointment that comes with living in this not-so-perfect world? Some girls might choose to let go of hope in favor of looking inward, living only for the moment and for themselves. But some shut out the world, assuming that by not interacting with other girls, they can avoid being hurt. Several others choose not to trust anyone else. These girls essentially place themselves as the "gods" of their own destiny.

The apostle Paul issued a challenge in Romans 8: We are not to give up hope; instead, we are to "eagerly wait for it with patience." Hope is a desire for a certain thing to happen and requires trust in someone or something apart from one's self. When you hope, you acknowledge that you can give your very best, but the outcome is still not totally up to you.

In our world, it's impossible to be patient without hope. For us to wait patiently, we have to hold on to the hope that the outcome will be better than the present moment. A Christian's hope is founded in our trust in a good, just, and faithful God. When hope starts to fade, look to God and strengthen your trust in Him.

delight |

Recall a time you were truly disappointed in your circumstances or in a girl you know. What role did a lack of hope play in your thoughts and behaviors?

How would a belief in someone bigger than yourself—who is in control of the future—change your outlook on that disappointment?

display |

Carefully read Romans 8:31-39. Do you realize how much God loves you? Whenever your hope seems to be fading, read these verses to help remind you that you can trust Him. Your belief in God will directly impact your trust in Him, and consequently, your ability to remain hopeful.

In a journal or on a blank sheet of paper, write out Romans 8:31-39, replacing every instance of "us" with "me." Personalize this passage and use it as an encouragement that God is with you and for you—no matter what's going on or who tries to stand against you.

> **Acknowledge your disappointments to God. Tell Him what you deeply long for but maybe don't have at the moment. Ask Him to strengthen your trust in Him when you are impatiently waiting for things to change.**

day 3

LOVE IS PATIENT

discover

READ 1 CORINTHIANS 13:1-5.

Love is patient, love is kind. Love does not envy, is not boastful, is not arrogant, is not rude, is not self-seeking, is not irritable, and does not keep a record of wrongs. —1 Corinthians 13:4-5

What girl doesn't want a friend that is patient, kind, does not envy, does not brag, and is not arrogant or rude? She is not all about herself, doesn't become irritated easily, and refuses to hold a grudge. This friend sounds amazing!

Jesus said that "whatever you want others to do for you, do also the same for them" (Matt. 7:25). Jesus (who is also God, by the way) thought this command was important—so vital to our faith life that it sums up "the Law and the Prophets." Basically, this one command is a summary of what God wanted His people to do and what the prophets called the people to return to doing!

We are all works in progress. We all need to show patience and have others be patient with us. Irritation and frustration will inevitably arise in your relationships, but in those moments, remember how wonderful it is when someone shows you patience.

"Love is patient." It's so very telling that when the apostle Paul (inspired by the Holy Spirit) wrote out a definition of love, the first word he chose to describe love was "patient." Patience is key to showing love to others and feeling loved by others.

delight

Think about how you like to be treated by the girls around you. What difference does patience make in how you like others to treat you?

How do you respond to other girls when they become irritable and easily angered? How can you show patience to them in those moments?

display

It is inevitable: You will become impatient with another girl this week (maybe even today). Consider how you can be more patient with her. Practice speaking a quick prayer before you respond to her, even if it's something as simple as, "Lord, help me right now." If it is a girl you have an exceptionally tough time loving, talk to a trusted, godly woman about your difficulties. Listen as she shares her experiences. Everyone struggles in this area, but it doesn't mean you should stop trying to show patience to others.

> Confess to God your impatience with others and when you don't love them as you should. Ask the Holy Spirit within you to help you love others no matter what. If one girl in particular is difficult for you to love, pray for her and ask God to teach you to love her.

In the Waiting

day 4

GOD'S CALLED PEOPLE

discover

READ EPHESIANS 4:1-6.

Therefore I, the prisoner in the Lord, urge you to walk worthy of the calling you have received, with all humility and gentleness, with patience, bearing with one another in love, making every effort to keep the unity of the Spirit through the bond of peace. —Ephesians 4:1-3

Consider this line from today's Scripture: "walk worthy of the calling you have received." What is this "calling"? If you look back to Ephesians 1:5, the apostle Paul said, "God predestined us to be adopted as sons through Jesus Christ." Girls, in the biblical context, sons received the blessings of their father's inheritance, and here, the term "sons" includes you! If you trust in Jesus, then God has called you into His family.

You did nothing to earn this position. It was given freely to you through Jesus' death and resurrection, yet God calls you to live in a way that is worthy of this high calling. These verses lay out for you what it looks like to be worthy of the designation as a child of God. This girl exudes qualities like humility, gentleness, patience, bearing with one another in love, and staying united in peace. Living this way reflects to the world the kind of God you serve.

When you choose to show patience with others, you are showing that you have a higher calling given by your heavenly Father. You are showing the girls around you that they are important enough to wait on. Hopefully, one day you'll get to share with these girls that God thinks they are important as well.

delight

Have you ever considered being patient part of a higher calling from God? How does that change your outlook on showing patience to others?

Take a moment to consider God's character in light of the fact that He desires His followers to be patient. Since God wants His children to be patient, what does that say about Him?

display

Now that you know being patient with others is part of a higher calling from God, imagine the moments when you lose patience. Consider the thoughts that run through your head as you grow impatient, irritable, and angry. Journal one way you will fight those thoughts with the truth that you have a higher calling than what is going on right at that moment.

> **Praise God that you don't have to meet a standard to be called one of His children. Thank Him for Jesus' sacrifice on your behalf. Pray that God will continue to add to you the qualities of someone worthy of being called a child of God.**

day 5

PRIDE VS. PATIENCE

discover

READ ECCLESIATES 7:8B-9.

A patient spirit is better than a proud spirit. Don't let your spirit rush to be angry, for anger abides in the hearts of fools.

The Book of Ecclesiastes was written by the wisest king ever to live—Solomon. In this book, he laid out what he discovered about living life well. He pointed out how so much of what we invest our time and energy in is not eternal. Solomon wrote that pride was a character trait of fools. To be prideful is to consider yourself more important than others; it's a desire to protect self rather than follow God's plan. Those who choose to continue to follow this path and reject God's instructions were called fools (Ps. 14:1). A foolish girl doesn't trust a good and sovereign God—she only trusts herself.

Solomon also wrote not to "let your spirit rush to be angry." Rushing to anger describes exactly how a proud person responds to conflict. A prideful girl wants to control, but a wise girl wants to understand. A wise girl is patient. She asks questions, tries to assess the situation from different viewpoints, and considers solutions that will benefit all involved in the conflict.

Solomon was a king who had it all—wealth, power, influence, and love. Yet his advice about living the good life is attainable for everyone: "A patient spirit is better than a proud spirit." It is astounding how such simple advice helps us so greatly toward living a satisfying life.

delight

Read Proverbs 15. List any observations you make on how to handle an argument with wisdom.

Consider your own life. Do you want to be a girl who trusts in God or who thinks she has all the answers without seeking knowledge elsewhere? What do your actions say about who you trust?

display

When you feel anger about to overcome you, stop. Consider how you can show patience to yourself or someone else. Try asking a question to gain understanding about the situation instead of assuming you know exactly what is going on. Write out a scenario where you can patiently pause and ask a clarifying question rather than pridefully assuming you understand and responding in anger.

> Pray that the Lord will show you your pride. Ask Him to humble you and to teach you patience. Confess any personal areas where you struggle to be patient or girls in your life you struggle to be patient with.

In the Waiting

The Vital Virtue of Patience

We all have our moments of impatience, whether we let our attitude show or not. Take a look at the following list and mark how impatient you would feel in this situation.

> 1 = "This is great!" 5 = "This is annoying, but I can handle it." 10 = "Why me?"

A younger friend, sibling, or neighbor keeps asking me questions, following me around, or copying everything I say and do.

1 2 3 4 5 6 7 8 9 10

My best friend hasn't responded to the text I sent her over an hour ago!

1 2 3 4 5 6 7 8 9 10

The dance is only a month away, and I still haven't found my dress.

1 2 3 4 5 6 7 8 9 10

I can't wait until I'm able to stay home by myself/drive/stay out later/other.

1 2 3 4 5 6 7 8 9 10

The girl in front of me at the coffee shop took a REALLY long time to decide what she wanted, then she ordered about 100 things. I feel like I've been waiting forever!

1 2 3 4 5 6 7 8 9 10

These days it seems everything is instant. The problem with an instant society is that not everything is *actually* instant, and that makes us impatient. But impatience is more than a negative attitude—it isn't healthy. Here's the thing: patience isn't just good for your physical and mental health, it's also biblical. God is fully aware of our humanity—He created us! He knew we would have our impatient moments, and He provided plenty of instruction for us about being patient in all things and with all people.

But how do we cultivate patience—especially for those difficult moments when we'd rather scream or sigh dramatically because we're still waiting?

Here are five key verses about cultivating patience in your life. Write out each of these verses on a note card, then, the next time you feel impatient, read one of your verses. At the very least, it'll give you something to do while you wait. But the important thing is, you'll be learning to hide God's Word in your heart—the key to responding to any difficult situation (Ps. 119:11).

> Patience is better than power, and controlling one's emotions, than capturing a city. —Proverbs 16:32

> With patience a ruler may be persuaded, and a soft tongue will break a bone.
> —Proverbs 25:15

> Now may the God who gives endurance and encouragement grant you to live in harmony with one another, according to Christ Jesus.
> —Romans 15:5

> Let us not get tired of doing good, for we will reap at the proper time if we don't give up.
> —Galatians 6:9

> My dear brothers and sisters, understand this: Everyone should be quick to listen, slow to speak, and slow to anger, for human anger does not accomplish God's righteousness.
> —James 1:19-20

day 6

PATIENCE FOR EVERYONE

discover

READ 1 THESSALONIANS 5:12-21.

And we exhort you, brothers and sisters: warn those who are idle, comfort the discouraged, help the weak, be patient with everyone. —1 Thessalonians 5:14

In this letter to the church in Thessalonica, the apostle Paul pleaded with the people to live a life that revealed what freedom in Christ looked like. He compared not knowing the grace and mercy of Jesus to being "asleep" or being in the dark. However, Paul explained knowing and experiencing that grace as being "awake" or in the light (1 Thess. 5:5-8).

Paul gave several instructions on what life looks like when people are "awake" and living in the light. He described a community of people who respect those who work hard, encourage and comfort one another, help those who are weak, and are patient with everyone. Could you imagine living with people who actually lived this way? What an influence this community of people would have!

Notice that Paul identified the recipients of each specific command: We are to warn the idle, comfort the discouraged, help the weak, and be patient with everyone. The instruction to be patient is to be given to *everyone*. Being patient is a part of being "awake"—a part of experiencing and knowing the love, grace, and mercy of Jesus. To be patient is a gift God allows us to use when we've experienced and known the patience of Jesus. We are free to let go of our controlling, impatient, and unhealthy patterns of life to be patient with others instead.

Lifeway Girls | Devotions

delight |

Do you believe that knowing the love of Jesus is freeing? Why or why not?

Consider how your life would be different if you saw God's command to be patient as a privilege rather than a burden. Give one example of how things might be different for you if you thought this way.

display |

Are there some girls who you find it easier to be patient with than others? This week, take notice of the girls you show patience to and the girls you don't. Try to understand your responses to these girls and talk with God about helping you find patience for everyone you encounter. Name one girl you need extra patience with and ask God to grant it to you.

> Ask God to help you view patience as a gift from Him and not a burden. Pray that He would keep you in His grace and continue the work of making you more like His Son, Jesus.

day 7

CHARACTER BUILDING

discover

READ ROMANS 5:1-5.

And not only that, but we also rejoice in our afflictions, because we know that affliction produces endurance, endurance produces proven character, and proven character produces hope. This hope will not disappoint us, because God's love has been poured out in our hearts through the Holy Spirit who was given to us.
—*Romans 5:3-5*

What an odd thing for the apostle Paul to write to Christians in Rome: "We also rejoice in our afflictions." No one ever associates rejoicing with affliction. Pain, suffering, and difficulties come with affliction—and none of those are reasons for rejoicing. Right?

The apostle Paul said the affliction itself isn't what leads us to rejoice, but what is happening to us *through* the affliction. Affliction produces character. Character is our inner strength to maintain our values and principles, even when it's tough. God wants you to have character. He wants you to be able to maintain what's most important when circumstances look bleak. This character produced in you as you endure tough things brings hope.

Hope is an amazing quality. People who are able to hope can cope so much better in life. Christians can hope with confidence that our God conquered even our worst fears when He demonstrated victory over death through Jesus. Christians have a different, enduring kind of hope because we follow a God who lives, and we know death is not the end.

delight

How do you tend to respond to difficulties* in your life? Do you endure patiently? Why or why not?

Describe one way you can patiently endure through a difficulty you're facing today. How can you maintain hope as you endure?

display

Do your own research on *hope*. Search online for the benefits of hope. Talk to women who seem genuinely positive and ask them what role hope played in their philosophy on life. Record your findings in your journal and start to implement hopeful thinking today.

> **Ask the Lord to be with you in your afflictions. Tell Him all your troubles; He cares for you (1 Pet. 5:7). Pray for His strength to help you endure.**

*You may want to talk to a parent, pastor, or a trusted, godly woman about your difficulties. God never said we are to endure alone. Some afflictions can be addressed by talking about what is going on with someone in authority.

day 8

THE LORD IS COMING

discover

READ JAMES 5:7-8.

Therefore, brothers and sisters, be patient until the Lord's coming. See how the farmer waits for the precious fruit of the earth and is patient with it until it receives the early and the late rains. You also must be patient. Strengthen your hearts, because the Lord's coming is near.

James, the brother of Jesus and early church leader, wrote these words to Jewish Christians who had spread throughout the world due to persecution (Acts 8:1). James wrote to people who were in danger of losing their lives and couldn't return home. If anyone needed encouragement, it was James' audience. He told them to "be patient until the Lord's coming." He knew this promise of Jesus' return was their greatest hope in dark times.

What are the signs of Jesus' return? They aren't exactly "good": anguish on the earth, people overwhelmed with fear, and people having to flee their homes (Luke 21:20-22). Looking back, we can see the impact this scattering of people from Jerusalem had on the world: the good news of Jesus Christ made its way to others who weren't in Jerusalem.

Through this scattering, many were introduced to Jesus for the first time—all because the people who scattered didn't give up hope. They patiently waited for the Lord to return. They told others about Him and His promises. Today, He is still working miracles for many to come to faith in Him before He returns.

delight

Have you ever felt abandoned by Jesus and all on your own? What thoughts did you experience? How did you deal with those thoughts and feelings?

Pay attention to your surroundings—your home, family, friends, opportunities, and so on. What are some signs that God might be blessing you right now?

display

Take some time to observe nature. Marvel at the sun, moon, and stars. Watch the insects as they build or work. Touch the morning dew on a plant and smell a flower. Nature is a great way to see God has not abandoned us.

> **Thank God for the beauty of His creation as a reminder He is still at work. Tell Him when you feel like He has abandoned you, and ask Him to remind you of His presence daily.**

day 9

HE HEARS

discover

READ PSALM 40:1-3.

I waited patiently for the Lord, and he turned to me and heard my cry for help. He brought me up from the desolate pit, out of the muddy clay, and set my feet on a rock, making my steps secure. He put a new song in my mouth, a hymn of praise to our God. Many will see and fear, and they will trust in the Lord.

Do you ever picture patient people as those who don't say anything and can sit quietly with hands folded in their laps for a long time? Psalm 40 gives us a different picture of patience. This psalm was written by David, who was recalling a difficult situation he encountered. He described this time as being in a "desolate pit."

David did not sit down in this pit and quietly wait for someone to help him out. He cried out for help! His waiting patiently involved prayer—fervent, meaningful, genuine, raw, and pleading prayer. God heard and delivered him. David wrote, "He put a new song in my mouth, a hymn of praise." It would seem that David's song prior to being rescued wasn't a song of praise. It might have been one of confession, groaning, and sorrow.

Let David, a man after God's own heart, shake any preconceived notions you may have about being patient. Being patient isn't always sunshine and rainbows. Being patient is clinging to God as if there is no other way out of your mess. It is crying to Him, telling Him what is wrong, and asking Him to do something.

delight |

David said he waited "patiently." Look at the description that follows. Is this how you would define waiting patiently? Why or why not?

How has reading Psalm 40 changed your idea of what patience looks like?

display |

Biblical patience is not denial of the need for a Savior. It's not distracting ourselves with things of this world until Jesus comes back; it's fervently seeking God for our problems right now. God is big enough to take on your complaints, difficulties, and cries. He wants to help you if you will just seek Him out.

Read Jesus' parable on prayer in Luke 18:1-8 and consider how you could be more persistent in your prayer life. Write out one idea of how to grow in your prayer life and act on it.

> **Start talking to God about your struggles. Push aside any preconceived ideas that "He doesn't want to hear my complaining" or "He has more important things to do than listen to me." Just open up to Him about what it is you're going through, and ask for His help.**

day 10

REMOVING HINDRANCES

discover

READ HEBREWS 12:1-2.

Therefore, since we also have such a large cloud of witnesses surrounding us, let us lay aside every hindrance and the sin that so easily ensnares us. Let us run with endurance the race that lies before us, keeping our eyes on Jesus, the source and perfecter of our faith. For the joy that lay before him, he endured the cross, despising the shame, and sat down at the right hand of the throne of God.

Trusting in God's promises, acting in obedience to Him, and then patiently waiting for your reward is not easy. The men and women in the Bible who are applauded for their faith clung to God no matter what. They continued believing God even when it meant facing catastrophic floods, leaving family and home, rejecting riches and power, and fighting seemingly impossible battles. The author of Hebrews compared this waiting to an endurance race.

Enduring the pain of a long race takes effort. Yes, God will help you and see you through, but you are not a passive participant. To run well, you must throw off anything that might hold you back and remain faithful. The Bible provides lists of sins and stumbling blocks as well as stories of people who have fallen, but you must examine your own life to learn what is hindering your faith. Then, you have to take action to remove it from your life.

Most importantly, you are to keep your focus on Jesus. Remember His promises of eternal and abundant life, to be with you and never forsake you, and to bring you into the family of God. These are your rewards for the taking if you will remain patient and faithful.

delight |

What might keep you from remaining faithful to God?

Look up John 3:16; 10:10; 14:27; and Ephesians 1:5. What are the rewards given to Jesus' followers if they remain faithful to Him?

display |

Take action against something holding you back from being faithful to God. If you feel stuck or helpless, talk to another trusted Christian or pastor for help. Don't expect big changes overnight, but write out one small step you can make right now.

> **Praise God for His promise of rewards. Ask Him to motivate your heart to remain faithful and to work to move aside anything that's holding you back.**

Let us not get tired of doing good, for we will reap at the proper time if we don't give up.

GALATIANS 6:9

day 11

WAITING ON OTHERS

discover

READ 2 PETER 3:9.

The Lord does not delay His promise, as some understand delay, but is patient with you, not wanting any to perish but all to come to repentance.

The apostle Peter wrote this letter to encourage believers in their faith. In chapters 2 and 3, Peter talked about people who spread lies in an attempt to turn believers away from their faith. He said that these people will reject God and tell His followers that He is not coming back. Peter warned Christians to not believe these lies.

He told them to look at creation instead. He said that people who reject God forget the world He created—and how it all came to be. Paul even said God's "eternal power and divine nature have been clearly seen since the creation of the world" (Rom. 1:20). These "scoffers," as Peter called them, ignore God's displays of glory, question His existence, and encourage people to doubt whether Jesus will really come back to save them (2 Pet. 3:3-4).

Jesus has good reason for "delaying" His return. He is being patient for all to come to Him—He will wait for His people to repent. His "delaying" is not to discourage you, but to allow others to come to Him in faith.

As Peter said, "With the Lord, one day is like a thousand years, and a thousand years like one day" (2 Pet. 3:8). For many of us, patience wanes when something takes longer than we'd like. For God, time is not that way. He has the patience to wait for even the most wicked of us to realize our need for Him.

Lifeway Girls | Devotions

delight

When do you tend to feel impatient with God?

Why might it be easier to wait when you know Jesus has a purpose behind His waiting?

display

Examine your faith. Do you truly trust that God is good and that Jesus will return? If you have doubts, talk to God about them. Find a few mature Christian women and ask them what doubts they have had and how they have dealt with them. Write out one doubt you struggle with and talk about it with one of these godly women.

> Praise God that He wants good for all. Acknowledge His goodness. Pray for God to secure your faith in Him even when others may question it.

In the Waiting

day 12

ALL GLORY TO HIM

discover

READ 1 TIMOTHY 1:12-17.

But I received mercy for this reason, so that in me, the worst of them, Christ Jesus might demonstrate his extraordinary patience as an example to those who would believe in Him for eternal life. Now to the King eternal, immortal, invisible, the only God, be honor and glory forever and ever. Amen. —1 Timothy 1:16-17

The great apostle Paul—who wrote most of the New Testament—had a dark past. He once persecuted the church. He invaded people's homes, arrested them, and dragged them off to prison if he found out they followed Jesus. (According to Acts 8:3, He was known as Saul at the time he was persecuting Christians.) Christians were terrified of Paul. For this reason, he called himself "a blasphemer, a persecutor, and an arrogant man" (1 Tim. 1:13).

But an amazing encounter changed everything for Paul: Jesus appeared to him in a blinding light and gave him a chance to stop his wicked ways and begin to follow God (Acts 9). Paul described his salvation as a gift of mercy from Jesus. He said Jesus displayed "extraordinary patience" with him.

Paul is not unique in receiving God's patient offering of salvation; it's offered to all who will follow Jesus. Salvation is not based on anything you have done or will do, but on the patient, merciful nature of God. When we see our salvation through this lens, we can't help but offer praise to the God who has been so good to us.

delight

Has your understanding of salvation been that it is all about your doing, or do you understand the mercy and patience of God on your behalf? Explain.

How can you give glory to God for your salvation?

display

Take time to consider one way you can show glory to God. Here are a few ideas: talk with a girl friend about God's impact on your life, sing a song of praise, or consider how you can serve others. Commit to doing that action this week. Write out how you'll give God glory for His patience with you.

> **Praise God for who He is, what He has done, and what He has promised to do in the future. Confess times when you haven't praised Him as you should, and ask for His help to acknowledge His patience with you.**

day 13

SLOW TO ANGER

discover

READ PSALM 103:8-13.

The LORD is compassionate and gracious, slow to anger and abounding in faithful love. —Psalm 103:8

The great King David of Israel wrote, "The LORD is slow to anger and abounding in faithful love." But David is certainly not the first or only person in the Bible who made this claim about God. God is actually the first One recorded as making this claim about Himself. As Moses went on Mount Sinai to receive the Ten Commandments, God said these words about Himself: "The LORD is a compassionate and gracious God, slow to anger and abounding in faithful love and truth" (Ex. 34:6).

It's astounding that the God who created the world and everything in it, who has all power, who can be anywhere at any time, and who knows everything, would choose to describe Himself as "slow to anger and abounding in faithful love"! It's because these are the qualities of His nature He wants you to know about foremost. It's important to God that you understand His nature—that whatever He does, He is slow to anger and abounding in faithful love.

In the verses that follow, David wrote about God's willingness to forgive and remove the sin of those who fear Him. His patience with His people is a demonstration of His faithful love to them. David compared God to a father showing compassion to his children. God wants us to know without a doubt that His nature is patient and loving.

delight |

What words would you use to describe God's nature?

Why do you think God chose—out of all His attributes—to say He was "slow to anger and abounding in faithful love"?

display |

Consider God's loving kindness to you. Decide how you can share that loving kindness with a girl you know. Write out her name and one way you can be patient and slow to anger when you interact with her.

> Thank God for His loving nature. Thank Him for His forgiveness of sins, abounding love, and relenting anger. Praise Jesus for taking the punishment of your sin on the cross so that you can be in a right relationship with God the Father.

In the Waiting

day 14

RENEWING JOY

discover

READ PSALM 30:5.

For His anger only lasts a moment, but His favor, a lifetime. Weeping may stay overnight, but there is joy in the morning.

King David, who wrote Psalm 30, was called "a man after [God's] own heart" (1 Sam. 13:14). He understood God's nature and exemplified it throughout his life; however, David was far from perfect. He made some atrocious mistakes. He had an affair with a married woman and had her husband murdered. His family life was a wreck as well. He had multiple wives and a son who had another one of David's sons killed.

David knew about God's anger. He faced several harsh consequences for his disobedience. However, we see David repent throughout his life when confronted with his sins. In Psalm 51, he prayed fervently for God not to leave him and to forgive him.

God forgave David and blessed him with a son, Solomon. God would establish an eternal kingdom through Solomon's descendant, Jesus (2 Sam. 7:11-13). David experienced both God's anger and His favor. He understood that God does not tolerate wickedness, but is willing to forgive all who genuinely repent.

God's anger is momentary, but His favor is for a lifetime. God's anger toward sin is real. If it wasn't, then Jesus didn't need to die on the cross. But His favor is so much greater than His anger. His anger will be satisfied and will come to an end, but His steadfast love for His people will never stop.

Lifeway Girls | Devotions

delight

Have you ever felt like God was too angry at you to forgive you? Explain.

Read Romans 8:31-39. What is your assurance that God's love for you will never run out?

display

Morning represents a new start. This morning (if you are doing this devotion in the morning) or tomorrow morning (if you are doing this in the afternoon or evening), write a journal entry about how grateful you are to receive His forgiveness. Ask Him to help you genuinely repent of sins and to get a fresh start. Ask Him to turn places of weeping in your life to joy.

> **Rejoice that God's anger is momentary, but His favor is for a lifetime. If you feel like God is angry with you, confess your sin to Him and plead for Him to remove it from you. Place your trust in Jesus' work on the cross on your behalf.**

In the Waiting

day 15

A REMINDER OF GOD'S GOODNESS

discover

READ LAMENTATIONS 3:22-33.

The LORD is good to those who wait for him, to the person who seeks him. It is good to wait quietly for salvation from the LORD. —Lamentations 3:25-26

Lamentations was written about the destruction of the city of Jerusalem. God warned the people this destruction was coming. They had been told multiple times that if they didn't turn from their wickedness, disaster was coming (Jer. 18:11-12.) Eventually, God did not protect them from the destruction of their holy city when the Babylonians attacked (Lam. 2:17). The city was destroyed, many were killed, and people's lives were left in ruin.

The difficulties that followed the devastation were intense. Families were dying and people were taking extreme measures to provide for themselves. All these tragedies surrounding the writer of Lamentations made his words more inspiring. He knew the Lord's discipline wouldn't last forever.

He was able to remain patient by reminding himself of God's goodness: "Because of the LORD's faithful love we do not perish, for his mercies never end" (v. 22). He understood God's desire was not to punish His people, but to redeem them. He saw this discipline as an invitation to draw near to God. Eventually, God brought salvation to His people, and not just to Judah, but to all who place their trust in Him (John 3:16-17).

Lifeway Girls | Devotions

delight

Imagine for a moment if you were never disciplined. How would you behave if there were no consequences for your actions?

Read Hebrews 12:3-13. What does this show about God's purpose for discipline?

display

We can't assume that every bad situation we encounter is God disciplining us for some sin we committed in the past. Sometimes bad things happen to us because other people sin or because we live in a world where natural disasters happen. Whatever the cause, it's important to remember God cares for you. Talk to Him when you are confused about why something horrible may be happening to you or someone you love, and remind yourself of His goodness. Memorize Lamentations 3:25-26 to help you focus on God's goodness even during difficult times.

> **Thank God that He cares enough for you to discipline you. Ask Him to help you remain faithful when you are going through tough situations.**

day 16

EVEN HERE

discover

READ JEREMIAH 29:10-14.

"For I know the plans I have for you"—this is the Lord's declaration—"plans for your well-being, not for disaster, to give you a future and a hope."
—*Jeremiah 29:11*

The nation of Babylon conquered Jerusalem. They deported the people and forced them to live in a foreign land. But God gave a word to the prophet Jeremiah to share instruction and encouragement with His people. God told them to continue living where they were. He told them to build homes, work, farm, get married, and grow families in Babylon (Jer. 29:4-7). He told them to seek good for the city where He placed them, even if it was not their home. He had a plan for them that might not have been what they imagined, but was certainly for their benefit. His plan for their lives didn't include them hanging on to the past or wishing for how things used to be.

Where you are right now may not be where you want to be. Maybe not all the conditions in your life are ideal. But God wants you to thrive. So, how are you to thrive even here? God has a plan for you to live out His kingdom in your life.

Jesus told us some ways to thrive in Matthew 5. He told us to be peacemakers, to be pure in heart, and to seek after righteousness. He told us to work out our anger with others, to not let our lust control our actions, and to remain committed in our relationships. It may seem simplistic, but these instructions are how we thrive until Jesus returns.

Lifeway Girls | Devotions

delight

Do you feel like you're not where you want to be in your life right now? How is that affecting your thoughts and behaviors?

How can knowing that God has a plan for your future be helpful in remaining patient when things aren't perfect?

display

Decide to stop wallowing in self-pity. Consider one small step you can take to thrive where you are. Think of something that would serve and build relationships with the girls around you. Once you take that first step, the others follow more easily. Write out a few ideas.

> **Thank God that He has a good plan for you. Praise Him that He is on your side and doing things for your good. Confess times when you felt forgotten, and ask Him to remind you of His presence when you feel like you've been left behind.**

The Lord is good to those who wait for him, to the person who seeks him. It is good to wait quietly for salvation from the Lord.

LAMENTATIONS 3:25-26

day 17

HIS WAYS ARE NOT MINE

discover

READ ISAIAH 55:6-9.

"For my thoughts are not your thoughts, and your ways are not my ways." This is the LORD's declaration. "For as heaven is higher than earth, so my ways are higher than your ways, and my thoughts than your thoughts." —Isaiah 55:8-9

Like Jeremiah, the prophet Isaiah wrote to the people of Judah who had been displaced from their homes and were residing in Babylon. They were devastated by what happened to their nation and discouraged about having to settle down in Babylon. But God wanted them to know that all was not lost. He invited them to come to Him.

In Isaiah 55, God told the people not to pursue things that don't satisfy. Instead, He told the people to come to Him for satisfaction. He called them to seek Him and to stop their wickedness, and He promised that He would forgive them. He reminded them that He was unlike them. He thinks and acts differently than we expect.

God is not always predictable. His nature is immutable—meaning it'll never change. God will always be loving and just, but you will not always be able to predict His patterns. We will probably be confused at times about what God is doing and what He is accomplishing. This confusion is because God is working a whole universe for His glory and our good. It's not always going to make sense to us in the moment, but we can rest assured He is in control and has a plan greater than we could ever imagine.

delight

In what areas of your life do you search for satisfaction apart from God?

How does it comfort you to know that God is unlike you in His thoughts and actions?

display

Spend some time examining where you place your satisfaction. It may be a relationship, a hobby, or an identity you have adopted. Ask yourself: *Is it sinful to continue after this thing?* If yes, then take action to stop pursuing it. If not, ask: *How can I put this thing in priority below God?*

On an index card or sticky note, write out the words *God above all*. Place this note where you'll see it often as a reminder that God should have the place of highest honor and importance in your life.

> **Confess when you have not sought God for your satisfaction and have pursued other things. Thank God that He is not like you. He does not worry or fret, but He is confident in His plan.**

day 18

A STRAIGHT PATH

discover

READ PROVERBS 3:5-6.

Trust in the LORD with all your heart, and do not rely on your own understanding; in all your ways know him, and he will make your paths straight.

This proverb was written from a father, King Solomon, to his son. The father told his son how to have a life that's full of joy and prosperous. His instructions were for the good of his son and to help his son avoid common pitfalls many others fell into. If he followed the instructions, he would have favor with men and God.

Solomon said to trust the Lord with *all* of your heart. He didn't give allowance for any half-way trusting. Life-giving trust in God is whole-hearted trust. As Jesus said, we are "to love the Lord your God with all your heart" (Matt. 22:37). Jesus called it the greatest commandment. In fact, Jesus said all of the law God gave stems from this central commandment, along with loving others as ourselves (Matt. 22:40). Needless to say, this one action of whole-hearted trust in God embodies just about everything God has for us to do.

Life as a teen can feel like times of tumultuous waiting for your "real life" to begin. You have so many important decisions to make in the upcoming years that will chart the course for the rest of your life. No matter the course you choose, you can't go wrong if you are trusting in God with all your heart. Seek Him for wisdom and make decisions based on what you understand to be the most God-honoring choice.

Lifeway Girls | Devotions

delight

Who do you turn to for help on tough decisions?

Have you ever made decisions merely based on what everyone else around you is doing? How did that decision turn out?

display

Consider a big decision you have to make in the near future. Write out what wisdom you have gained from God's Word that might pertain to the decision. Talk to godly girls and women you trust who are faithfully following Jesus. Ask them what insight they might bring to this decision.

> **Talk to God about the decisions that are weighing on you. Ask for His wisdom in those situations. Thank Him for giving you His Word and the church for insight on how to find wisdom outside yourself.**

day 19

LIFE'S INTERRUPTIONS

discover

READ ACTS 16:6-10.

After he had seen the vision, we immediately made efforts to set out for Macedonia, concluding that God had called us to preach the gospel to them.
—*Acts 16:10*

The Book of Acts was written by a doctor turned missionary named Luke. He described a particular journey in Acts 16 where Paul was prohibited by God from entering a certain location. Paul was not one to shy away from difficult circumstances. He continued to preach in places where he knew he could be persecuted and possibly murdered (Acts 14:19-20). So, Paul wasn't making excuses by saying the Holy Spirit forbid them to go there.

After being told not to go to Asia or Bithynia, Paul received a dream that led him to go to Macedonia. Apparently Macedonia was not where Paul planned to go next, but God had other plans. It would seem that bringing the good news of Jesus would be beneficial for any location, so why was God so adamant about going to Macedonia? Sometimes God throws a detour in what seems to be a good path. Remember, His ways are not our ways. But Paul remained faithful wherever he went, and we should do the same.

Unplanned turns will happen on everyone's journey in life. It is what we do when those turns happen that really matters. Don't let detours throw you off God's plan to bring about His kingdom wherever you go and through whatever you are doing. Remain patient and trust in Him.

delight

Has God stopped you from pursuing an opportunity or a relationship even though you felt sure it would work out great? How did you react?

What might you be missing out on when you choose your own way instead of God's way?

display

C. S. Lewis once wrote, "The great thing, if one can, is to stop regarding all the unpleasant things in life as interruptions of one's 'own', or 'real' life. The truth is of course that what one calls interruptions are precisely one's real life—the life God is sending one day by day: what one calls one's 'real life' is a phantom of one's own imagination."[2] Read over this quote a few times slowly. Decide today to let the interruptions that come your way be welcomed as God's way of giving you a new opportunity.

> **Tell God about the times you've been disappointed by plans that have failed. Ask Him to renew your confidence that He has not abandoned you. Pray for Him to continue to guide your steps for your good and His glory, even if it is painful.**

day 20

IT'S NOT ALWAYS ABOUT YOU

discover|

READ ACTS 16:11-15.

A God-fearing woman named Lydia, a dealer in purple cloth from the city of Thyatira, was listening. The Lord opened her heart to respond to what Paul was saying. —Acts 16:14

After God interrupted Paul's plans for travel, Paul ended up in a town called Philippi. In his time there, he looked for people who were already seeking after God. He wanted to tell them about Jesus. Remember, Jesus had only been crucified and resurrected 40 years prior, and news did not spread as fast as it does today. Paul's traveling to those places brought life-changing information. His words gave direction and meaning to their entire lives.

One such person was Lydia. Notice that the Bible described her as "a God-fearing woman." Lydia believed in God and wanted to know Him better. Paul's words gave her that fulfillment. Her faith in Jesus even spread to everyone in her household. She was so appreciative of Paul's work that she opened up to her home to him.

People all around you are looking for encouragement, words of hope, and meaningful relationships. Sometimes we can't see that in others because of our own hangups. Maybe we're upset because life took a turn we didn't plan on. Whatever the reason, the circumstances you find yourself in are not always about you and your personal goals. There might be a bigger reason God has you where you are. To find out why, strive to use whatever circumstance you're in to bring glory to God.

delight

When have you been guilty of making others around you miserable just because you feel miserable? Explain.

How have you seen positive people make a difference in others' lives?

display

Name a girl in your life who needs some encouragement. Think of an action you can take to encourage her and be a good friend. It doesn't have to be big. It could be something as simple as slowing down, asking how her day is going, and then listening. Consider how you can make that girl feel important this week. Write out a few ideas.

Whether this action makes it on your list or not, consider taking the time to handwrite a note of encouragement to this girl. Share with her one of the verses from this devotional that has encouraged you.

> As you seek to be an encouragement to others, it will be essential that you keep coming to God for your own personal encouragement and fulfillment. Ask Him to "fill you up" so that you can go and share confidently with others about your relationship with Him. Pray that even if you face rejection, you won't take it personally, but that you'll continue to be patient and care for that person.

day 21

EXPECT OPPOSITION

discover

READ ACTS 16:16-24.

Bringing them before the chief magistrates, they said, "These men are seriously disturbing our city. They are Jews and are promoting customs that are not legal for us as Romans to adopt or practice." The crowd joined in the attack against them, and the chief magistrates stripped off their clothes and ordered them to be beaten with rods. —Acts 16:20-22

Just because God purposely placed Paul in Macedonia didn't mean there would be no opposition. One day while they were ministering in the city, a demon-possessed slave girl who could predict the future confronted Paul and his friends. When Paul cast the demon out of her, it really put a damper on her owner's earnings. They wanted him to pay for their loss of income, so they took Paul to the government authorities and made false accusations. Paul took a severe beating for his faith and was thrown into prison.

It's tough to compare the opposition we might face for our faith to Paul's. However, the severity of the opposition Paul faced doesn't downplay the opposition you may face today. There are countless people, cultural messages, and personal insecurities that may discourage you and seek to stop you from continuing in your faith.

Opposition comes in so many forms, and it's important to not compare your struggle with someone else's. You are called to continually seek to honor God in whatever you do. Paul revealed a beautiful model of how to persevere and endure when facing opposition. He never gave up or lost hope.

delight |

What kind of opposition to your faith do you face most often?

How might your attitude toward opposition change if you expect it instead of being surprised by it?

display |

Identify some opposition you face in sharing your faith with others. Think through the consequences of remaining silent. What might happen if you decide to take a risk to share anyway? Write out a plan of how you will respond the next time you face opposition for your belief in Christ.

> **Pray for confidence in your faith. Ask God to guard you against any opposition that would cause you to lose hope. Pray that you are strengthened in the midst of your opposition and not frightened.**

day 22

GOD DELIVERS

discover

READ ACTS 16:25-34.

About midnight Paul and Silas were praying and singing hymns to God, and the prisoners were listening to them. —Acts 16:25

After being humiliated and beaten in public for proclaiming their faith, Paul and Silas were put in jail. They weren't the kind of men to be deterred by adversity. They weren't giving up in their journey to spread the news of Jesus to everyone they encountered. The Bible says that even while they were in jail, they were praying and singing hymns to God, and the other prisoners were listening.

God sent a violent earthquake that shook the jail—all the prison doors opened, and the prisoners' chains were loosened. God came through for His people once again. He provided an escape when things looked bleak.

The Philippian jailer was about to take his own life, thinking his prisoners had escaped. But Paul always sought to save as many people as possible. Even though the doors were opened and his chains were loosened, Paul stayed, talked the jailer out of suicide, and told him about Jesus.

In Romans 12:12, Paul gave advice to others about what to do in tough times. He said to "be patient in affliction." Paul demonstrated in that Philippian jail what patience looks like—trusting and praising God no matter what. He knew every situation he found himself in was ordained by God. He was where God wanted him, and he used that time to share Jesus with others.

Lifeway Girls | Devotions

delight

How can you show more patience to others when you are feeling impatient?

How does knowing that God is taking care of you help you have more patience with others?

display

When you feel like being impatient, stop and take a deep breath. Consider how you can value the girls you interact with when you feel like moving on to the next thing or being somewhere else. Take time to say something like, "I'm about to go do something else, but before I do, is there anything you need from me?" When you make a practice of asking these kinds of questions, you will be surprised how much the attitudes of the girls around you will soften and relax.

> Ask God to help you value people over your own agenda. Ask Him to teach you how to be patient with others when you'd rather be doing something else. Thank Him that He took the time with you to hear your prayers and be there for you.

Now to him who is able to do above and beyond all that we ask or think according to the power that works in us—to him be glory in the church and in Christ Jesus to all generations, forever and ever. Amen.

EPHESIANS 3:20-21

Section 4: HOW TO BE PATIENT

day 23

PRAYER

discover

READ PHILIPPIANS 4:6.

Don't worry about anything, but in everything, through prayer and petition with thanksgiving, present your requests to God.

After Paul's arrest, beating, and imprisonment, a group of Philippian believers worshiped together in a local church that Paul planted. It is to this church that Paul wrote these words. He expressed his care for the people and his desire to see them firmly rooted in Jesus.

Worry happens when we allow our minds to focus on the wrong things, like our struggles and anxieties.[3] You may think worrying is not a choice. Anxious thoughts just seem to pop in your head automatically. But the choice to continue to focus and dwell on that thought is yours. Worry is what sticks around when you don't stop your anxious or negative thoughts.

The answer for worry is prayer. Talk to someone who can actually help with what you are worried about. Jesus said, "Come to me, all of you who are weary and burdened, and I will give you rest" (Matt. 11:28). He can help with whatever you are going through. His help may not be what you expected, but He promises to never leave you, and in the end, you won't be disappointed (Rom. 10:11; Heb. 13:5). When you allow your anxious thoughts to remain, you are choosing to make yourself unhappy. Your heavenly Father wants to help you. He wants you to bring your concerns to Him for your happiness and His glory.

Lifeway Girls | Devotions

delight

What are some anxious thoughts or worries you struggle with?

How can you develop a habit of turning worries over to God in your daily prayer life?

display

When you have an anxious thought, talk to yourself. Say "stop" either in your mind or aloud. Try speaking truth from God's Word to your fears and anxieties. Then, take that same worrisome thought and make it a prayer right then. Keep up this ritual of saying "stop" and turning the thought into a prayer until it becomes a habit.

> Confess your anxious tendencies. Thank God that He wants to care for you and that He listens to your concerns. Praise Him that He is faithful to guide you.

day 24

SLOT TO SPEAK

SLOW TO SPEAK

discover

READ JAMES 1:19-21.

My dear brothers and sisters, understand this: Everyone should be quick to listen, slow to speak, and slow to anger, for human anger does not accomplish God's righteousness. —James 1:19-20

James' advice to his readers was that they should be "quick to listen, slow to speak, and slow to anger." We all like to feel heard. We all want someone to think about their response before they speak, and we don't want others to rush to anger after we have expressed our thoughts and opinions.

Jesus followers must understand that anger won't accomplish the change of heart in a person that only God can bring about. People may stop a behavior if you get angry with them, but heart change (which is what God is all about) happens through the Holy Spirit.

God's Word tells us that "A gentle answer turns away anger, but a harsh word stirs up wrath" (Prov. 15:1). Your anger with someone will not bring you closer; it will only stir up harsh feelings. Every relationship has tense times when conflict arises. It's only when we reconcile and apologize that relationships are strengthened—not when we yell, name call, or assume the worst about others. Leaving conversations with both parties angry can lead to bitterness and resentment that can last years. A simple apology after a fight can go a long way toward building the kind of friendships that can last a lifetime.

delight

How do you like to be treated by others? Do you feel calmer when the person you're talking to is quick to listen?

How do you usually handle conflict? Are you able to listen and talk calmly without letting your anger take control? Explain.

display

Arguments are inevitable, and although it's better not to lose your temper in the first place, it happens. Is there a girl you need to go to and apologize for losing your temper? Go and apologize to her. Do your part to repair the relationship as best you can. If you can't, give her some space, and try again later.

> **Thank God that He is quick to listen, slow to speak, and slow to anger. Ask Him to help you to be like Him in your quickness to listen, slowness to speak, and slowness to anger.**

day 25

A SIGN OF COMMITMENT

discover

READ HEBREWS 6:13-20.

And so, after waiting patiently, Abraham obtained the promise.
—Hebrews 6:15

The writer of Hebrews was concerned for those who might be tempted to leave the faith. He told the people to hold on to the promises of God. The ones who remain faithful and patient receive the rewards God offers (Heb. 6:12). The writer then gave an example of someone who embodied this truth—Abraham.

God made a great promise to Abraham in Genesis 15 that Abraham's offspring would be as numerous as the stars. God revealed the permanence of His commitment to this promise by having Abraham cut animals in half. God then passed through the animal halves.

Having someone pass through slaughtered animals as a sign of commitment may seem like an odd ceremony for us today, but it meant something very significant back then. Whoever walked through the animal halves was essentially saying, "If I break my promise to you, may I be like these animals." It was a very serious commitment, and God meant every bit of it. Abraham believed God, and the Bible says God counted his belief as righteousness.

Your sign that God is committed to His promises to you is His Son, Jesus. Jesus' death and resurrection is the evidence that God will also conquer death in you and you will live forever with Him. Will you trust His promise?

Lifeway Girls | Devotions

delight

Do you have a difficult time believing that other people will keep their promises to you? Why or why not?

What are some of the promises you have read about in Scripture that God has made to you?

display

Look at your list of Scriptural promises. Reflect on how you would think and behave differently if you truly believed these promises were true every moment of your life. Start believing and adopt thoughts and behaviors that reflect the reality of these truths. Jot down one way you will put this into practice today.

> **Claim God's promises for yourself. In your prayers, remind God of His promises to you. God is not forgetful, but He does appreciate you speaking His Words back to Him. Thank Him for Jesus' death and resurrection as His symbol of promise to you.**

day 26

FOR YOU

discover

READ EXODUS 14:5-14.

But Moses said to the people, "Don't be afraid. Stand firm and see the LORD's salvation that he will accomplish for you today; for the Egyptians you see today, you will never see again. The LORD will fight for you, and you must be quiet."
—Exodus 14:13-14

The Israelite people had been enslaved by the Egyptians for over 400 years. These people didn't even know a life apart from slavery. They had been crying out to God to rescue them for years. The Egyptians were cruel taskmasters, and God's people suffered under them. Finally, God sent Moses to rescue the people out of Egypt. God sent plagues that destroyed the Egyptian water, land, animals, and people until Pharaoh released the Israelites.

As they were leaving, Pharaoh changed his mind and wanted the people back. He gathered an army of hundreds of men and chariots and rode after the Israelites. Understandably, the Israelites panicked. They blamed Moses and began to wonder if an enslaved life might have been better. All the while, God never left them. He was still fighting their battles for them. All He asked of His people was to trust Him to deliver them.

As Jesus told His disciples just before His arrest, "You will have suffering in this world. Be courageous! I have conquered the world" (John 16:33). Jesus has guaranteed us victory through Him. We just have to trust in Him to quiet our worries and believe His Word is true.

delight

What are some ways your panic shows up in your behaviors?

How can knowing that God has everything under His control help you handle situations that could cause you to panic?

display

Memorize Ephesians 3:20-21. When you feel yourself starting to panic, take a deep breath and repeat these verses to yourself over and over. Remind yourself that this world is not all there is to your life and that you serve a powerful God who fights on your side.

> **Praise God for fighting your battle of sin and death through His Son, Jesus. Spend time asking Him to calm your fears and give you rest for your soul.**

In the Waiting

While You Wait

God doesn't operate on our timetable because He exists and works outside of time as we know it. So, it can seem like we spend a lot of time waiting for God to move. In reality, He's preparing us for what's to come in His perfect timing.

The Bible is full of examples of godly men and women who spent a lot of time waiting. Some waited their entire lives to see a promise come to fruition, and others were patient even without seeing any "proof." Look at the list of names and Scripture passages on the left and draw a line to match them with how the person revealed patience while waiting on the Lord.

Abraham and Sarah
(Gen. 12:1-3; 18:9-15; 21:2-4)

Leah
(Gen. 29;30; 31)

Ruth
(Ruth 2; 4)

Hannah
(1 Sam. 1)

Zechariah and Elizabeth
(Luke 1:5-25; 57-66)

Anna
(Luke 2:36-38)

He was 100 years old when his son was born. His wife laughed when God told her she would have a child.

She lost her husband, then followed her mother-in-law to a new land. She gathered excess crops from a relative's field until he became her kinsman redeemer.

For years, she prayed for a son, but remained childless. She promised God that if He gave her a son, she would dedicate him to serve the Lord. God answered her plea with a son, Samuel.

She was barren, and they were both "well along in years." When an angel told him they would have a son, he didn't believe it, so he couldn't speak until his son was born.

Her father tricked her husband into marrying her, and she struggled to feel loved. Yet, she continued to trust God and praise Him for each child He gave to her.

She faithfully served God in the temple, day and night. She fasted and prayed. When she met Jesus, she spoke of the redemption of Jerusalem.

While each of these men and women waited for God to fulfill His promises to them or waited on the Lord to move them out of heartbreaking circumstances, we see one key factor over and over: God was with them in the waiting. He met each one of them right where they were, and He does the same for us.

We may not ever see the result of our efforts, the resolution to a certain issue, or healing in a specific relationship, but we can wholeheartedly trust that God is moving and working in our lives whether we see His hand actively or not.

In fact, take a look at Hebrews 11. If you write in your Bible or use a Bible app, highlight every time you see the words "by faith." In the Christian Standard Bible, the phrase occurs 22 times in this passage! These men and women were patience pros. They lived their lives fully and vibrantly for the Lord, all without seeing the promise completely fulfilled in Jesus.

By faith, will you trust God, too?

Spend some time reflecting in prayer. In what area of life are you struggling to be patient or wait on the Lord to move? Journal your response.

day 27

FLEE FROM EVIL

discover

READ 2 TIMOTHY 3:1-9.

People will be lovers of self, lovers of money, boastful, proud, demeaning, disobedient to parents, ungrateful, unholy, unloving, irreconcilable, slanderers, without self-control, brutal, without love for what is good, traitors, reckless, conceited, lovers of pleasure rather than lovers of God, holding to the form of godliness but denying its power. Avoid these people. —2 Timothy 3:2-5

The apostle Paul wrote this letter to his "spiritual son" Timothy. Paul had discipled Timothy and given him a place of leadership in a church he started. Paul wrote this letter to help Timothy be prepared for how life would look as they waited for Jesus' return.

The description of people's behaviors in the last days wasn't pretty. These characteristics describe someone who has chosen to serve herself over God. She traded in serving the God who sent His only Son to reconcile all people to Himself for momentary pleasure and self-gratification.

There are several lists throughout Scripture of the characteristics of a genuine believer in Christ. Galatians 5:22-23 is one such passage, explaining that "the fruit of the Spirit is love, joy, peace, patience, kindness, goodness, faithfulness, gentleness, and self-control." These are the characteristics we should chase after. They are characteristics that honor God, show His nature to the world, and honor others as valuable. A girl who has these traits builds authentic relationships with others and glorifies God with her life.

delight |

As you read over 2 Timothy 3:2-5, do you feel convicted about any of those characteristics for yourself?

Why do you think it would be a good idea to not be surrounded by people who practice these kinds of behaviors?

display |

You may feel you aren't measuring up to the descriptions of a Christian and that your life sounds more like the description of a person the Bible says to avoid. Don't be discouraged! Sometimes in the process of becoming more like Christ, we see our sin more clearly, and it feels like we are failing when actually we are making real progress. So, rejoice that you want to make a change, and keep going!

> **Praise God that He doesn't leave you as you are but is continually working on your character. Ask Him to help you make tough decisions about the people you allow to influence your life. Pray that He would keep you on the path to growing to be more like Jesus.**

In the Waiting

day 28

FOLLOWING IN PATIENCE

discover

READ 2 TIMOTHY 3:10-13.

But you have followed my teaching, conduct, purpose, faith, patience, love, and endurance. —2 Timothy 3:10

In these verses, Paul commended Timothy for following his example. Timothy showed himself to be a faithful friend and dedicated disciple. Paul met Timothy on one of his missionary journeys. Fellow believers told Paul what a great person Timothy was, and Paul found their reports to be true (Acts 16:2). After meeting Timothy, Paul decided to take him along on his other journeys, and they worked together to instruct numerous others in the way of Jesus.

But Paul was not Timothy's first mentor. Timothy's mother and grandmother were also believers. We don't have many details about these women, but Paul called their faith sincere (2 Tim. 3:5). Timothy's faith and conduct were marked and shaped by the examples he chose to spend his life following—Paul, his mother, and his grandmother.

The example of those we choose to follow will mold our character. Timothy was able to grow by following the examples before him. Paul is not here today for us to follow, but he and other faithful people have left writings to encourage us and inspire us to follow their teaching, conduct, faith, love, endurance, and patience.

delight

How could being around a patient person help you be patient with others?

Other than following an example of someone you know personally, how can you find examples to help you grow your character?

display

As you think about who you follow (and not just on social media), consider their influence on you. Decide who you want to be in five years, ten years, and twenty years. Start surrounding yourself with girls who will help you on that path. Also, be aware of relationships in which you are a positive influence. Make an effort to be the kind of girl you want others to imitate. Name one girl or woman whose faith you would like to imitate.

> If you already have a spiritual mentor, thank God for that woman. If you don't, ask God to bring one into your life. Also ask God to show you a girl you can be an example of godliness to.

day 29

THE POWER OF GOD'S WORD

discover

READ 2 TIMOTHY 3:14-17.

All Scripture is inspired by God and is profitable for teaching, for rebuking, for correcting, for training in righteousness, so that the man of God may be complete, equipped for every good work. —2 Timothy 3:16-17

There is power in the words of God. Power to give life, power to heal, and power to reveal the very intentions of our hearts (Heb. 4:12). We are able to get a better picture of our desires, thoughts, and wants as we read the Word. It will show you the patterns in your life that are keeping you from what God has for you and the patterns that will give you abundant life.

Paul told Timothy that the Scriptures are profitable for teaching, rebuking, correcting, and training in righteousness. All of these words lend themselves to images of one person coaching another. God's Word is like your personal trainer for spiritual fitness. It tells you the exercises to prepare for God's work in your sphere of influence.

When you are seeking to be more patient with yourself or with others, let the Word be your guide. You will find encouragement to keep pursuing patience, examples of others who modeled patience, and words of warning against impatience. Since God's words are powerful enough to create the world and bring the dead to life, they can certainly change a stubborn heart into a patient and loving one.

delight

Share about a time when someone's words had a powerful affect on you. How so?

Do you believe in the power of God's Word? Why or why not?

display

You are almost finished with this exploration in patience. Spend some time finding your next devotion. Commit to studying your Bible every day for the next 30 days. As you study, journal thoughts as you have them and changes you observe the Lord bringing about in yourself.

> Thank God that He left you His words in the Bible. Pray that He will transform you to the image of His Son as you study His Word.

day 30

OUR HOPE IS IN

discover

READ PSALM 37:7-9.

Be silent before the LORD and wait expectantly for him; do not be agitated by one who prospers in his way, by the person who carries out evil plans. Refrain from anger and give up your rage; do not be agitated—it can only bring harm. For evildoers will be destroyed, but those who put their hope in the LORD will inherit the land.

The great King David of Israel wrote these words to encourage others to maintain their hope in God. One of their biggest distractions (and probably yours too) from waiting on God was when they saw someone else prosper. When we see others doing well who we know are not waiting on God, it makes us want to quit what we are doing and go after what others have.

David's advice is to "wait expectantly for him." To wait expectantly means you trust God to do something. It's not the kind of waiting that waves a white flag and accepts a life of disappointments. It's the kind of waiting that is optimistic that your situation is only temporary and that things will change in time. It's the kind of waiting that builds your relationship with God—not the opposite.

The bottom line is that you will need to exercise patience when others prosper while you don't, but your patience is grounded in a God who cares for you. He wants you to succeed. He wants you to achieve great things, but they will only come about through His ways and His timing. Only those who maintain hope will receive the promised rewards.

delight

Describe a time when you felt that you deserved what someone else had.

What became of your feelings? Did it hurt your relationship with that person or with God?

display

Review Romans 8:31-39. Journal about how you know God wants the best for you. (Hint: The answer is in verses 31-32). Also, take note about what will separate you from the love of God. Describe how being reassured of God's goodness and love can help you wait on Him.

> Confess times when you grew angry over others' success. Bring any concerns of your own failure to God. Ask for His help to remain faithful to Him while you wait.

In Pursuit of Patience:
Six Steps to Help You Overcome Irritation and Choose Love

Breathe.
When you find yourself feeling impatient—with a person or situation—remember to breathe. Sometimes we're tempted to hold our breath until resolution comes, but that is neither healthy nor recommended. Taking a deep breath in and slowly exhaling can actually slow your heart rate from its irritated pitter-patter to a normal rhythm.

This would also be a good moment to pray for patience. Despite what we might think, asking God for patience shouldn't be some flippant request of "Lord, help me not to go off on this girl!" Praying for patience focuses on your heart being right before God. Ask Him to soften your heart toward Him and others, then ask Him to help you continue to grow in His likeness—including having His heart for patience.

Retreat.
Remember this: You're human, and you won't get it right every time. But with God's help, you can handle more than you might think. You can have extraordinary patience. By listening to the Holy Spirit's guidance, you might determine that the best course of action is to retreat. This doesn't mean you never address the issue; it simply means you're taking a step back from the moment to refocus on the big picture. When we have the opportunity to remove ourselves from a stressful situation, we can often return to the conversation later with a clear head and calm heart.

Perceive.
Whether you're breathing or retreating, take a good look at your perception of the person or event. In the moment, we tend to respond emotionally to stressful situations, maybe as a result of feeling attacked or because our stress level is already seriously high. When a girl does something that offends you or accuses you of hurting her, tap into your perception of events. Try to look at the situation as an outsider and ask yourself some key questions:

- What am I currently going through that might be coloring my perception?
- Is there any truth to her accusation? If so, how can I address her issue in a godly way, even if I don't appreciate the way she presented it?
- If there's no truth to her accusation, ask yourself: What might she be going through that could make her feel stressed/anxious/angry?

Set Your Mind and Focus Your Heart.
Our mindsets and the focus of our hearts greatly affect our response to difficult

situations. If we want to respond in God-honoring, Christ-centered ways, then our minds need to be set on His Word and our hearts focused on Him. Even in the middle of tough stuff, we can't lose sight of the One who matters more than everything and loves us all more than anything.

Praying for patience is often reduced to a humorous quip or caution not to pray for patience as if God would punish you by then making you wait. Here's the truth: Things were always going to happen in God's timing, and they always will. So, don't be afraid to pray for patience. While part of praying for patience is getting your own heart right before God, we also need to remember who it is we're praying to. Approach God with praise for His character and thank Him for the way He loves us. When you've done these two things, your heart is in the right place to pray for the other person.

Respond.
If you need to retreat from a situation, be sure to communicate your heart plainly to the other person. You might say something like, "Thanks for coming to me about this, _____ (name). I know that wasn't easy. I want to honor you in my response, so I'd like some time to think over what you've said."

If it seems that she's just having an off day or there's something going on, perceive the mood in the room (asking the Holy Spirit for guidance here is key). Consider asking: "Hey, _____ (name), it sounds like you're having a tough day. How can I help?" If she's a fellow believer, offer to pray with her.

Only God knows the motives of our hearts, so we might not understand why people do what they do, but we don't have to. God calls us to love as He loves us (John 13:34), and sometimes the most loving response we can have is to say and do nothing—refuse to fuel the fire anger feeds. Remember that no response is a response, too.

Trust God.
No matter what the situation or how well or imperfectly you handled things, trust God with the outcome. We cannot control anyone's response but our own, and we can only do that through the presence and guidance of the Holy Spirit. Trust that God loves you and this other person immensely, and regardless of what it might seem like in the moment, He cares so much about what you're going through. Throughout Scripture, we see His faithfulness, kindness, goodness, and love for people. We can trust that He has everyone's best interests at heart.

Challenge: Commit to implementing these steps next time you have a conflict with someone. In a journal or notebook, write about that experience. Then, write out a prayer for that girl.

In the Waiting

notes

notes

Endnotes

1. Neil Patel, "The Psychology of Instant Gratification and How It Will Revolutionize Your Marketing Approach," Entrepreneur, June 24, 2014, https://www.entrepreneur.com/article/235088#:~:text=Instant%20gratification%20is%20the%20desire,hard%20to%20practice%20%E2%80%94%20delayed%20gratification.
2. Trevin Wax, "C.S. Lewis on Life's Interruptions," The Gospel Coalition, February 26, 2011, https://www.thegospelcoalition.org/blogs/trevin-wax/c-s-lewis-on-lifes-interruptions/.
3. "Worry," Merriam-Webster (Merriam-Webster), accessed March 19, 2021, https://www.merriam-webster.com/dictionary/worry.